Butterflies and Moths: All about Butterflies and Moths, a Kids Introduction to Butterflies and Moths– Fun Facts and Fantastic Photos!

TABLE OF CONTENTS

INTRODUCTION

Thank you for purchasing the book *"Butterflies and Moths: All About Butterflies and Moths, A Kids Introduction to Butterflies and Moths–Fun Facts and Fantastic Photos!"*

With the help of this book, you will learn more about some of this world's most beautiful and amazing creatures: Butterflies and Moths! From their life cycles to different varieties, you'll surely have fun learning about these living beings. Plus, there are amazing photos for you to see and enjoy, too!

Start turning the pages now and get to know these creatures even more.

Once again, thank you and enjoy!

Butterflies and Moths: All about Butterflies and Moths, a Kids Introduction to Butterflies and Moths— Fun Facts and Fantastic Photos!

ENJOYING AND UNDERSTANDING BUTTERFLIES:
THE LIFE STAGES OF A BUTTERFLY

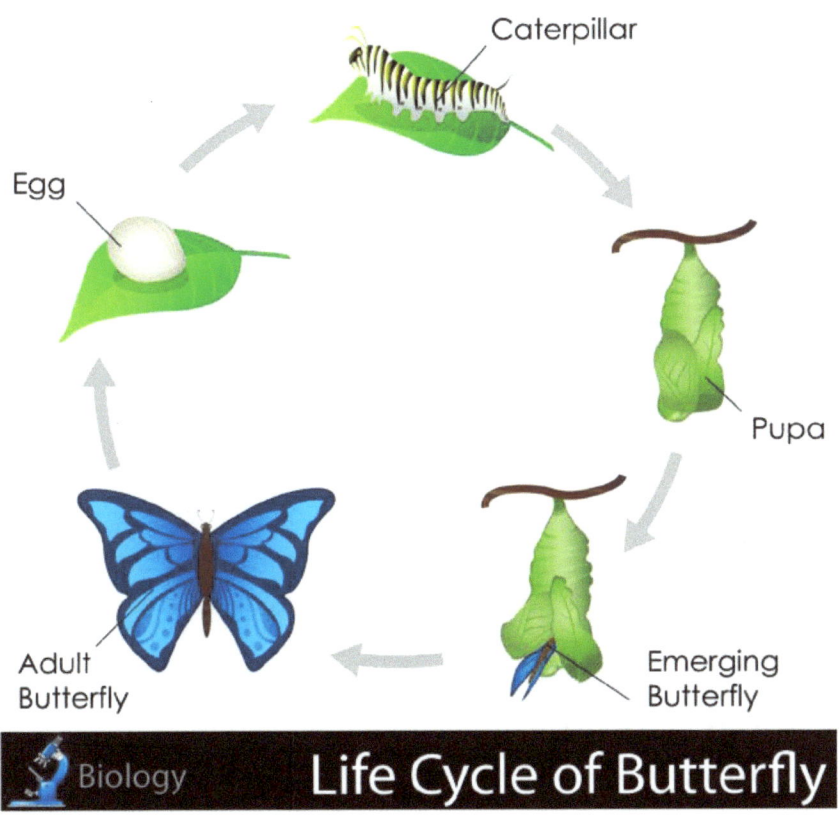

There are four basic stages in a butterfly's life. Here they are:

1. Egg

Adult Butterflies lay eggs on plants and are usually laid during spring, summer or fall. Butterfly eggs are almost invisible as they are extremely small.

2. Caterpillar

After the eggs hatch, then emerges the Larva, commonly known as a Caterpillar. The Caterpillar's main job is to eat enough so that the butterfly they become may grow up to be healthy and strong. A Caterpillar can grow up to 2 inches or even longer in just a week.

3. Pupa

When the Caterpillar has already eaten everything it needs to survive, it then becomes a Pupa (also called Chrysalis). It is during this time that the caterpillar waits to become a butterfly. It can stay as a Pupa for months. You can usually find Pupas on trees hanging upside down to camouflage itself against evil insects.

4. Adult Butterfly

And finally, the adult Butterfly emerges. It has colorful wings, long antennae, a compound set of eyes and of course, the ability to fly! The adult Butterfly's main job is to mate with other adult Butterflies and lay eggs—so that there will be more Butterflies for you to see in the future.

BUTTERFLY COLORS

There are over 20,000 different species of butterflies in the world, giving us the special opportunity to be able to enjoy them in a variety of beautiful colors. Butterflies offer some of the most vibrant and striking displays of colors in nature. They are simply beautiful.

A fascinating fact about butterflies is that their colors are usually not from pigments but are rather the effect of refraction, iridescence or diffraction. When the butterflies attract light, they are able to give off different colors, which are called **structured colors.** Peacocks, mother of pearls and some varieties of fish have the same quality.

However, there are also some butterflies whose colors are pigmented already—this is called Ordinary or **Pigmented Color.**

PUDDLING, COURTING, BASKING, AND EGG LAYING

There are also certain behaviors that are natural to butterflies. It's fascinating how they go forth with their life while doing these things.

Puddling

Butterflies get the nutrients they need by drinking still or shallow water. While you may think this is strange, it's actually beneficial for butterflies as these types of water are able to get minerals from the soil that butterflies need to live. Sometimes, butterflies also try to suck from the soil when there is no water around. This behavior is called **puddling.**

Courting

Male and Female butterflies take turns courting each other, depending on the season. Most of the time males use their "eye-spots" or those round spots on their wings that look like eyes to get a female's attention during dry season. They also beat their wings for the females to hear them. This is their way of calling the females.

Meanwhile, female butterflies with brighter spots often take the lead during the wet season. They lead males to places where there are loads of food sources causing the males to be attracted to them.

Basking

Since butterflies are cold-blooded creatures, it is extremely hard for them to generate heat on their own, especially during cold or rainy seasons when they may easily be prone to getting cold or chilling. **Basking** happens when butterflies sit on a patch under the sun with their wings outstretched so their internal temperature can be heightened.

Egg-Laying

Adult butterflies often lay eggs on the underside of a plant or a leaf. This is in order for baby caterpillars to easily be able to feed on the leaves and become healthy individuals. Butterflies are also able to attach eggs to the plants by a glue-like substance that they emit. The adult butterflies don't spend too much time with their offspring; rather they leave them alone to fend for themselves.

HOW TO REAR BUTTERFLIES

Rearing butterflies is the act of taking care of butterflies on your own! Or at least, taking care of baby butterflies before they get the chance to fly out and see the world. Yes, you can actually do it, but make sure that you will give these butterflies all your love and care and ask your parents or guardians to help you out.

First, you need a **rearing habitat**. An aquarium, terrarium or wide-mouthed jar could definitely work. You have to make sure that the rearing habitat has plant vases made from film and some plants where pupas can hang when this stage occurs. Plants are also needed as caterpillars feed on them. Sticks and stones should also be placed inside.

Steps in Rearing Butterflies:

➢ **Collecting Eggs**. Cut the leaves where you found the eggs and put them in the terrarium. Make sure that they are kept in glass-topped boxes or containers for them to easily be handled.

➢ **Caring for Caterpillars**. Caterpillars are pretty much independent—all they need are leaves to feed on and they're all good.

➢ **Pupa Care**. During this time, caterpillars will descend to the cage's floor (soil) and wrap themselves in leaves. Just leave them be and make sure that there is still an abundance of leaves in the terrarium.

➢ **Butterflies!** You'll know that the butterfly is coming when the pupa becomes darker. Watch as the pupa cracks and see the butterfly slowly emerge from it. Be careful not to be noisy, so that the butterfly will not be scared.

IDENTIFYING MOTH

While butterflies and moths have the same life cycle (eggs, caterpillars, pupa, adult moth), there are also some differences that would help you understand what is a butterfly and what is a moth. Here are some of them:

Anatomy

➤ Moths have Frenula which hold the forewing and hind-wing together; butterflies do not have these. Frenula are meant to make it easier for moths to fly.

➤ Moth caterpillars often just look like twigs as they are often brown while Butterfly Caterpillars are colorful and hairy and may resemble a leaf.

Wings

➤ When butterflies' wings are folded, they resemble vertical-shaped objects while moths' wings often resemble a tent that hides their abdomens.

➤ Butterflies' wings are larger and more colorful, while moths often have drab-colored wings.

Behavior

➤ While butterflies often fly during daytime, moths are nocturnal and are more comfortable in roaming around at night.

Chrysalis

➤ A butterfly's cocoon is hard but smooth and has no silk covering whereas a moth's cocoon is often brown and wrapped in silk.

THE BUTTERFLIES

Tiger Swallowtail

While it doesn't run like real tigers do, the Tiger Swallowtail butterfly is a very fast flier. It is also known for its black and yellow markings and its wings also have "tails" that are similar to that of the bird, swallow.

88 Butterfly

The 88 Butterfly is popular because it has the number "88" imprinted on its wing. It is often dark brown or white with metallic blue, red or black linings. They are fond of eating dung or rotten fruits. Yikes!

This butterfly is considered as a sign of good luck and is often found in Mexico, the Andes and Amazon.

Japanese Emperor Butterfly

The Japanese Emperor Butterfly is one of the biggest butterflies out there. It has a greenish underside with black and white spots. Males are differentiated from females by a blue spot or iridescence on their wings.

Blue Triangle Butterfly

Commonly found in Sydney, Australia, this butterfly's wings resemble a triangle and that's how it got its name. It also quickly moves from flower to flower to aid in pollination. The Blue Triangle Butterfly is one of the most helpful butterflies on the planet.

Apollo Butterfly

Named after the Greek God Apollo, the Apollo Butterfly loves flowering plants, especially thistles. They often live in grasslands or steppes and are exposed during different periods of the year, making them some of the most elusive butterflies ever.

Queen Alexandra's Birdwing

Rightfully called a Queen, this is the biggest butterfly in the world as its wings can grow up to a foot wide. Queen Alexandra's Birdwings are often found in the rainforests of New Guinea and are part of the endangered species list of the United States.

Blue Morpho Butterfly

The Blue Morpho has bright blue wings with black linings and is great in the art of camouflage, especially when insects and birds are around. When it flies, it gives other animals the vibe that it is appearing and disappearing so it's hard for them to keep track of it. The Blue Morpho is commonly found in Mexico and Colombia.

King Butterfly

Also called "Monarch," it is said that the King Butterfly is one of the most beautiful species of butterflies out there. King Butterflies are also known for flying for thousands of miles and migrating to Mexico and California during the cold season as the previously mentioned places have warmer weathers that butterflies can benefit from. You'll easily recognize the King Butterfly because of its orange and black pattern. Male Monarchs are larger than females, while females have darker patterns.

Ulysses Butterfly

Named after one of the most popular Greek characters of all time, the Ulysses butterfly is also one of the most prominent butterflies in the world. You'll easily be able to spot it as it resides in all continents with the exception of Antarctica. They are also easily seen because their bright blue color makes it effortless to get your attention.

Blue New Guinea Birdwing

The New Guinea Birdwing is the largest species of butterflies in Australia. Males have black and emerald spots on their blue wings while females have black and white spots. They often feed on seeds called the Native Dutchman's Pipe which is considered poisonous to humans. They can also be found in Indonesia and in the Cape York Peninsula.

Metallic Satyr

Unlike most butterflies that are colorful, this one most resembles a moth since it is often in the colors brown, gray, silver or black. They are also low-level fliers unlike butterflies that can fly high. The Metallic Satyr Butterfly is also sometimes called a "Wood Nymph".

Green Spotted Triangle Butterfly

Often found in Australia (and even featured on some of their postage stamps), this butterfly is either black or brown with many green spots which makes it almost invisible while in the rainforest.

Clearwing Butterfly

The Clearwing Butterfly is especially fond of the scent and look of Heliotropes—these are the only things that can get them out of seclusion. Since their wings are transparent, they can easily "disappear" or blend with the plants and trees in the forest.

Brimstone Butterfly

These **species** are known for their leaf-shaped wings. They live in woodlands and grasslands and are often found in hedges by the road. It is often said that the word "butterfly" actually came from "butter-colored fly" which is the color of brimstone.

Rice Paper Butterfly

The Rice Paper Butterfly is common in Southeast Asia and is a cousin of the King Butterfly. It is called as such because of the transparency of its wings, and the fact that rice is a staple food in Asia which shares the same color with this butterfly.

Banded Morpho Butterfly

The Banded Morpho Butterfly is also called the Achilles Butterfly and is often found in Paraguay and Colombia. It likes to eat rotting fruits and the sap of trees and often roams around with other Morpho Butterflies at night. Also, because it is quite small, it is often thought of as a moth.

THE MOTHS

Madagascan Sunset Moth

The Madagascan Sunset Moth is considered as one of the most beautiful and appealing moths on the planet. Its wings are iridescent, just like some butterflies' wings are, and it is also fond of flying during daytime which is not common to most moths. It is endemic to Madagascar and is often found from March to October.

Spanish Moon Moth

The Spanish Moon Moth is a very rare moth that butterfly and moth enthusiasts are fond of trying to find. While it is a larva, the Spanish Moon Moth resembles twigs and when it is fully grown, the wings are green and start to show an intricate pattern. It feeds on mosses, enjoys when the weather is warm, and is quite delicate and not easy to take care of. They are best left outdoors as there are only a few of them left.

Luna Moth

The Luna Moth's wings can reach up to 4.5 inches which makes it one of the largest moths in North America. It is easy for the Luna Moth to make itself look like a leaf as it is lime-green in color. Adult Luna Moths emerge during the months of June or July and can also be found in Canada and Florida. Adult Luna Moths also lay more eggs when the weather is warmer as they like it better than colder weather.

Wasp Moth

This moth is often thought of as a wasp because it imitates the look and colors of a wasp. This is in order for it to be safe from predators. These wasp moths are dangerous to fruit trees as they can inflict damage by boring holes on them. The adults often feed on nectar and pollen.

Giant Comet Moth

The Giant Comet Moth can be found in the rainforests of Madagascar and its wings can reach up to 20 centimeters wide. It is one of the largest silken moths around. One amazing thing about the Giant Comet moth is that during the pupa stage, the cocoon makes numerous holes so that the caterpillar inside will not die from drowning.

Tailed Silk Moth

The Tailed Silk Moth is considered a graceful flier and that's why it is one of the most appealing moths in the world. It is fond of flowers, especially Hydrangea—as pictured above— and often flutters around your windows at night, especially if you live in North America. Beware of this moth, as its spines can sting. Ouch!

Ghost Moth

The Ghost Moth also called white witch, great owlet moth, birdwing moth, moon moth, and several other names is often referred to as the world's largest moth in terms of documented wingspan, measuring more than 30 cm (11 13/16 in). The ghost moth moves so fast when it flies making it virtually undetectable during the day. It also rises and falls on the ground to attract females. When it is still a larva, it feeds on cultivated and wild plants and is even used in plant nurseries to feed on insects such as ants or mosquitoes.

Day Flying Moth

Just like real hummingbirds, the Hummingbird Hawk Moth is a day-flying moth which feeds off the nectar and pollen of flowers. It also hums audibly which makes people and other insects think that it is a real hummingbird so it keeps itself safe from harm. These moths are commonly found in Britain, especially during the summer and are highly fond of flowers like buddleia and honeysuckle.

Atlas Moth

The female Atlas Moth is the largest moth in the world in terms of wingspan. Its wings reach up to 12 inches wide and it is called as such because of its large size. Some say that it is called Atlas based on Greek Mythology, when Zeus said that the moth should carry the weight of the world on its shoulders. It is also popular for having what appear to be snakes on the side of its wings. Unfortunately though, the Atlas Moth only lives for 1 to 2 weeks.

BUTTERFLIES AND MOTHS FUN FACTS

Some awesome things you should know about moths and butterflies!

➢ While they are quite colorful, butterflies actually cannot see colors except for Red, Green and Yellow.

➢ A butterfly's wings are made out of Chitin, a protein that is found in the exoskeletons of insects which makes them transparent and really light. Their wings are actually their exoskeletons!

➢ While you use your tongue to taste different kinds of food, butterflies and moths use their feet to smell and taste food! This is why it is said that while butterflies look good, its unhealthy for you to let them trample on your food as you never really know where their feet have been.

➢ There are actually more moths than butterflies in the world. Butterflies only make up 6 to 11 percent of flying insects whereas moths make up 89 to 94 percent of them!

➢ When the Woolybear Caterpillar's bands turn black, it means that winter is actually just around the corner.

> When the temperature is less than 85 degrees, moths and butterflies cannot fly. This is why it is important for them to be in warm climates.

> Butterflies and moths actually cannot chew food — they only suck or drink them. This happens through proboscis or the emergence of a straw-like item from the moth or butterfly's mouth.

> A butterfly cannot fly right away after it emerges from the pupa. It has to wait for a couple of hours so that its body will become hard and dry before it could be able to fly. This happens so that its veins can pump blood to its wings and allow the butterfly to see the world.

> There are no butterflies or moths in Antarctica. You guessed right: because moths and butterflies do not like cold weather!

> The Brimstone Butterfly lives for 9 to 10 months, the longest lifespan of butterflies around the world! Most butterflies only live for a maximum of 2 to 4 weeks as

adults.

> ➢ Some moths actually do not have wings—they only crawl with their feet their whole lives.

> ➢ In Taiwan, the Atlas Moth is usually made into a purse because of its colors!

> ➢ Butterflies and Moths can actually carry things that are 50 times their own weight.

> ➢ Butterflies and Moths may lay one egg or up to a hundred eggs in one sitting!

LEARNING HIGHLIGHT: 10 QUESTIONS

Here's a little test to prove that you have truly been reading and that you understood what you read. Ready? Let's do this in 1, 2, 3!

1. Which butterfly is commonly found in Sydney and has wings that resemble a triangle? It is also pictured below.

2. Which moth bores several holes onto its cocoon so that the caterpillar inside would not die?

3. Which butterfly is commonly found in Southeast Asia and is named after an Asian Staple Food?

4. What is the largest moth in the world that also has snake-like heads on its wings?

5. Where does a butterfly often lay its eggs?

6. What do you call the process in which butterflies drink water from shallow streams or even from the soil for them to get the nutrients that they need in

order to live?

7. The 88 butterfly is fond of eating rotten fruits and _____? (Don't try eating this! It's highly dangerous—and icky!)

8. Which butterfly is fond of flowering plants, especially thistles? It is also named after a Greek God.

9. Which moth looks and acts like a wasp to protect itself from predators?

10. Named after one of the fastest-running animals in the world, this butterfly cannot run but can certainly fly real fast. What is it?

GLOSSARY OF TERMS

- **Camouflage**: This is the method of concealing or blending oneself into the environment to be able to be protected from enemies. Most insects do this as a form of defense mechanism.

- **Endangered:** Species that are endangered are soon to be gone from earth, or are in danger of extinction and that's why they should be allowed to live freely.

- **Frenula:** A group of bristles that hold the wings of certain insects, such as moths and make it easier for them to fly. These are twig-like structures in the body of insects.

- **Heliotropes:** Heliotropes are fragrant purple flowers that are cousins of Roses.

- **Imprint**: To imprint means to make a sign on a surface.

- **Invisible:** Not easy or even impossible to see.

- **Iridescence**: Iridescence is having the quality of being bright and is also about playing with colors. This is what happens to the wings of butterflies and what makes them colorful.

- **Migrate**: To migrate means to move from one place to another, such as from one region or country to the other and stay on the place you moved to for a while. This is what most butterflies do during winter season.

> **Pollination**: This is the process of transferring pollen from flower to flower. When this happens, seeds are formed and reproduction in plants occurs — making sure that there are more flowers and plants for you to enjoy as long as you live.

> **Prominent:** To be prominent means to be popular or known by many.

> **Purse**: Wallets or small bags.

> **Species**: Any organism belonging to certain categories such as humans, insects or plants.

> **Steppes:** Steppes are grasslands that are commonly found in Europe and Asia.

> **Transparent**: To be able to transmit light or to have an extremely fine texture that it is easy to see through it, just like the wings of butterflies.

CONCLUSION

Thank you again for purchasing this book!

I hope you enjoyed reading about my book on *Butterflies and Moths: All about Butterflies and Moths, a Kid's Introduction to Butterflies and Moths — Fun Facts and Fantastic Photos!*

I hope you enjoyed learning about moths and butterflies and enjoyed seeing their pictures, too! Now, you have something to share with your friends!

Finally, if you enjoyed this book, please take the time to share your thoughts and **post a review on Amazon**. It would be greatly appreciated!

Thank you!

A Note about the Author:

Sean Liburd is a father, husband, entrepreneur, community builder, educator, listener and thinker. He is the founder and co-owner of Knowledge Bookstore which was established on December 18, 1997. Sean has learned that books educate and inform - but they also make you laugh, wonder and carry you to worlds you've never heard of inhabited by people you've never seen - a kaleidoscope of cultures painted on the pages in words, in pictures and in dreams. Books "Awaken the Mind" which is both Knowledge Bookstore's slogan and Sean's goal.

Feel free to contact Sean Liburd at sil@gmail.com

Check out my Amazon profile here:

www. amazon.com/author/seanliburd

www.ingramcontent.com/pod-product-compliance
Lightning Source LLC
Chambersburg PA
CBHW050829290526
45792CB00001B/322

* 9 7 8 1 5 0 1 0 2 3 5 7 6 *